DON'T FEED THE PONIES

DON'T FEED
THE PONIES

ADDRESSES TO CHILDREN

by

IAIN HUTCHESON

Minister of Gilcomston St. Colm's Parish Church, Aberdeen

LUTTERWORTH PRESS, LONDON

First published 1971

ISBN 0 7188 1794 X

PRINTED IN GREAT BRITAIN
BY EBENEZER BAYLIS AND SON LTD.
THE TRINITY PRESS, WORCESTER, AND LONDON

CONTENTS

CONTENTS

BIBLE REFERENCES

BIBLE REFERENCES

I

DON'T FEED THE PONIES

I AM sure you have all heard about the famous ponies of the New Forest. These are wild ponies— wild in the sense that they do not live in stables, nor do they pull carts or wear any harness. They live and breed out in the open and are free to roam where they will. But they are not wild in the other sense of being dangerous. In fact they are very friendly animals and are great favourites of family parties as they pass through the New Forest. You just need to stop for a moment and the ponies will soon be browsing round you looking for titbits to eat. Who could refuse to give something to these friendly beasts? But you must refuse!

All along the roads of the New Forest are warning signs, "Do not feed the ponies." Why? For their own safety! The ponies have become so accustomed to being fed by passing motorists that they now keep near the main roads. With traffic as heavy as it is today, the ponies are in constant danger of being killed or injured. For their own good we must not feed them by the roadside. We must be cruel to be kind.

This often happens with humans too. For their own good we have sometimes to appear to be cruel and heartless. Often you have wanted sweets and Mother has refused to let you have them—not because she grudged buying them but for the sake of your teeth. This works out in far more important ways. Rules and regulations are laid down for us and we often object to them; we want to please ourselves what we do. If everyone was allowed to please himself, life would become unbearable. For our own good we just cannot go through life pleasing ourselves.

People sometimes say that being a Christian means "Don't do this" or "Don't do that" all the time. It doesn't, of course, but when we realize the real reason for some of the "don'ts" we can understand that they are for our own good and for the good of others.

If we try to follow the example of Jesus, if we carry out His rules and regulations, we will find life is much better for ourselves and for others. In the Bible we have the Ten Commandments which are rules and regulations given to us by God. Jesus explained to us why we should keep these commandments—because, if we love God and our fellowmen, we will want to do only what is good for them and for ourselves.

Perhaps the New Forest ponies cannot understand. But surely you and I can?

Proverbs 13:24

2

CENTRAL HEATING

WOULD you like to live in a house that has central heating? Just imagine going to bed on a cold night without shivering or feeling your feet are freezing. Or not having to rub your hands together because you are sitting doing your homework in the corner of the room furthest from the fire. Perhaps you are one of the lucky ones who live in a new house with under-floor heating. What a difference it makes! How modern and up-to-date it is!

Yet the Romans were doing it 1900 years ago. If you go to the town of Bath, you will find a house that was centrally heated when the Romans occupied this country. There are bubbling hot springs and the boiling water was led under the floors of the other rooms so that the whole house was heated.

What we think of as a modern solution to a modern problem was the answer found by the Romans.

We often find this in history. The difficulties we have to face are the same kind of difficulties earlier generations had to face. Very often our answers are the answers they found, too.

This is very true about the problems of living. I am not thinking just about things like central heating and houses, but the problems of people. How they live together, how they treat each other, how they behave themselves—the things we sometimes call "personal relationships". Or there are the problems inside each one of us. The temptation to tell lies, to cheat, to be unkind or selfish or greedy or ungrateful. These are our problems and we often think of them as new problems that need a new, modern answer. That is where we are wrong!

These problems, too, were solved over 1900 years ago by Jesus. He came into the world to show us how to overcome such difficulties. To give us His example to follow. To show us how to live with one another and with ourselves. He not only solved these problems 1900 years ago but promised to help us with our difficulties, and He is ready to do that for us today if only we ask Him.

It would be silly to refuse to use central heating today because the Romans used it 1900 years ago. It is even more silly to refuse to accept Jesus' answers to our problems because we think they are old-fashioned. He is offering to help each one of us today. With His help we can live together in love and brotherhood and make the best use of our lives. Let us accept this old answer to our modern problems.

Psalm 79:13

3

BY ROYAL APPOINTMENT

HAVE you ever noticed the royal coat of arms outside a shop? If you have, you will also have seen
the words "By Appointment to H.M. The Queen". In
the towns and villages near the royal palaces you will
see such signs above grocers and drapers, ironmongers
and fishmongers, bakers and hairdressers. These are
the shops used by the Queen and they are naturally
very proud of the honour and privilege of using the
words "By Royal Appointment".

I am sure you would all like to serve the Queen in
this way. You would all like to think that the service
you have to offer, the work you have to do, is of such
high quality and craftsmanship that it merits a "Royal
Appointment". You would be very proud of this
honour and privilege and do your best to be worthy of it.

Do you realize that you hold a "Royal Appointment"
at this very moment? Jesus is the King of Kings and He
has appointed each one of us to serve Him. This is the
greatest honour and privilege any of us can receive.
Jesus thinks you and I are worthy of His appointment
and is ready to use us in His service. We therefore must
do our best to be worthy of His trust.

You may wonder what a boy or girl can possibly do

for Jesus. Remember we are His hands, His feet, His voice in the world. He has given to us the task of making His world a better place. We have the job of helping people to live together in friendship and peace. Each one of us has a part to play in spreading abroad the love of Jesus. "By Appointment to Jesus" we must try to serve Him in this way.

The Queen's Appointments carry the royal coat of arms and are easily recognized. Those appointed by Jesus do not carry a coat of arms or a badge, but they, too, should be easily recognized. The helping hand, the ready smile, the friendly word, the understanding sympathy—these are the signs which indicate the "King's Appointment". These show people that we have been appointed by Jesus "whose we are and whom we seek to serve". Be proud and eager to serve Him at all times.

Ephesians 6:13

4

ATLANTIC BRIDGE

DO you know you can cross the Atlantic in less than a minute? You look surprised but it is true, and you need not travel by super-jet or even by fast liner but simply on foot.

ATLANTIC BRIDGE

If you ever spend a holiday in Oban on the west coast of Scotland, you will probably go for an outing to the Islands of Seil and Easdale. Eventually you will come to a bridge across what seems to be a small river and there you will see lots of people taking photographs of the bridge across the Atlantic. The bridge joins the island to the mainland and the little strip of water is part of the Atlantic Ocean. In this way many people cross the Atlantic without realizing it.

This reminds me of the difference between good and evil, right and wrong. Often when we think of evil, we think of something big like the Atlantic Ocean. We would not dream of taking such a big step as murder, or robbing a mail train. These things are so big that we feel quite safe; they are not the kind of things we are ever likely to do. They are not the kind of things we might accidentally get involved in.

Yet sin and wrongdoing often start in a small, small way. We do not deliberately set out to sin but, like crossing the Atlantic by a tiny bridge, we often do it before we realize it. We tell a small lie, we keep something that does not belong to us, or we are envious of others. Such things may seem unimportant by themselves but they usually lead to something more serious.

We must always be on our guard against being led into temptation. The only sure way is to obey the teaching of Jesus and try to follow His example. He warned His disciples that it was not enough just to keep from committing any of the big sins like murder; it was just as wrong to think about people in an evil way.

Remember, sin can happen so easily. It can be a big

thing like the Atlantic Ocean between America and Britain, or it can be small and apparently insignificant like the small strip of water flowing under the Atlantic Bridge. It may be some wrong we deliberately do, or something we do without realizing it was wrong until after it has happened. In either case it is still sin; it is still wrong, and we as Christians must be on our guard to avoid it at all times.

Matthew 5:21

5

TAKING CARE OF OURSELVES

ONE of the tests for the Gold Award in the Duke of Edinburgh's Award Scheme is a fifty-mile hike. To win the award, boys must be able to take care of themselves on this long journey. They must do their own cooking. They must find their own way there and back. They are expected to get away from the main roads, cutting across hills and away from the familiar routes.

This calls for a healthy body to be able to withstand the long hike and the varying weather conditions. It calls for a healthy mind, able to think for itself and meet any difficulties that may occur. The boys must depend on maps to plan their journey and on a compass to keep them going in the right direction.

I like to think of life as a hike on which we have to

take care of ourselves. For the journey of life we must try to have a healthy body to stand up to the strains of working and playing. We must also have a healthy mind to know what is right and wrong and to take advantage of all the gifts God has given to us.

On this journey, however, we are not left without some help. God has given us a map, a book of directions to show us where we should go. It is the Bible and in it we find God's plan for our journey; in it we are warned of the dangers and the pitfalls; by using it we can map out our hike through life. God has also supplied us with a compass—our conscience—which tells us if we are going right or wrong. Even when the hills of this world are shrouded in mist, our conscience, like a built-in radar system, keeps us on the right path.

Above all, God has given us a Guide who knows all the danger spots along the way and can lead us in the safe paths. He is always by our side as we journey along the hike of Life and with his help we cannot go wrong. That Guide is Jesus.

If you keep your body and mind healthy and active, use the Bible to plan out your journey, pay attention to the Compass of your conscience, and follow closely Jesus your Guide, then the highest of all awards, the commendation of God, will be yours at the end of life's great hike.

John 16:13

6

MUD ON THE HEADLIGHTS

NOT long ago I had to make a long journey by car, and wanted to return home the same day. In the morning when I set out it was very wet, and my windscreen wipers were working all the time until I reached my destination. During the afternoon, when I was attending to my business, the weather cleared, and by the time I set out for home it was a lovely evening. By the time I was half-way home darkness had fallen, so I switched on my headlights—and nothing happened! There was only a faint glimmer of light on the road before me. I felt annoyed with my garage people for not checking my battery before I left, but there was nothing I could do about it other than keep close to the side of the road and travel very slowly. I literally crawled home. I eventually arrived at my house about two hours later than I had expected and I was very annoyed when I went to sleep that night.

In the morning I took the car out, ready to give the garage people a telling-off, and, in the bright daylight, do you know what I found? There was nothing wrong with my battery, there was nothing wrong with my lights, but the front of my headlamps was thickly crusted with mud. The light could not shine through for the mud I ought to have wiped clean the day before.

Boys and girls, the Bible tells us that Jesus is the Light. So often, when things go wrong and we are left groping in the dark, we blame Jesus. We think He has let us down, yet it is our own fault. We have allowed the bad things in our lives to keep His light from shining through. We have mud on our headlights.

In another way, Jesus expects us to be His lamps shining clearly in the world. He wants to shine through us into the lives of others, but again little light gets through because of mud on our lamps. Instead of a clear beam shining before us, all others can see is a very dim glow.

Let us then make sure nothing prevents the Light of Jesus shining clearly into our hearts and our lives, and that nothing we do or think or say will prevent the Light of Jesus shining through us into the lives of others.

John 8:12

7

DEMOLISHING OR BUILDING?

THE other day I stood watching one of those wonderful machines they use for demolishing buildings. A man was sitting in the cabin of the machine and by pushing certain levers he was able to tear down the floors inside the old building and push down the walls. By using another lever he made the machine scoop up boulders, rubble and timber, and pour them all into a lorry to be taken away. I only stood for a few minutes, yet in that short time whole buildings disappeared.

On the other side of the street, building operations were in progress, but here was a different story. Many men were working, and day by day, bit by bit, for months and months, new houses were being erected. This was a very slow job in contrast to the demolition. It is always far easier to knock down than to build new; it is far easier to break than to mend.

This applies not only to things but to people. You attend church or Sunday school week after week. There you are learning bit by bit about Jesus and His teaching. Slowly but surely your character is being built—a Christian, that is, Christ-like character. It takes a long, long time, not just days, or weeks, or months, but years.

Yet this character can be broken or damaged in a few minutes. Angry words, selfish thoughts, nasty actions can undo the teaching of many months. It is easier to knock down than build anew. The damage you may do in a few moments of thoughtlessness may take many months to repair. The life that is ruined by carelessness may take years to recover.

The only safeguard is to have not just the teaching of Jesus but Jesus Himself. He can guard us against the things that destroy our hearts and lives—pride, temper, jealousy and greed. He not only guards us against these things but helps us to keep on building that good, new character Jesus wants all His followers to have.

A house that took months to build can be knocked down in a day. A character that took years to build can be destroyed in a few moments. With Jesus' help we can keep on building our lives according to His plan for us.

2 Corinthians 5:17

8

CAR LIGHTS

HOW many lights are on a car? It all depends on the size and make of the car, but at least there are in the front two headlights, two dipped lights, and two sidelights. There are also two amber lights called trafficators. At the back there are two red stop lights, two red brake lights and of course two more amber lights. There is also a light to show the car number in the dark. Inside the car there can be all sorts of lights, some just to let the passengers see what they are doing, some to show the driver the time or the speed at which he is travelling, and even some warning lights that show up when something is wrong with the car.

Let us look at some of them again and see if we need them in our own lives.

The most important lights are the headlights which show the motorist the way along a dark road. Life itself can be a dark road but Jesus said: "I am the Light of the World: he that followeth Me shall not walk in darkness." As we journey along the road of life we must always be grateful for the Light of Christ. We find that light in His life and teaching and only by following that light can we hope to reach our destination of full manhood.

Then there are the warning lights. When we apply the brakes on a car the red lights warn others that we are slowing down. On the panel in front of the driver there are other warning lights which tell that something is wrong. We need warnings in life too. When we are tempted to do wrong, the Ten Commandments and the teaching of Jesus warn us of the dangers, and inside us there is always our conscience shining brightly to guard us against evil.

When we are following another car we are grateful if the other driver shows us clearly what way he is going, and we too help when we do the same. So in life we are grateful to those who give us wise counsel and, by indicating where we are going, we may help others.

The last light I want to mention is the one that lights up the car number plate. This is necessary to identify the owner. It seems to say: "I am not ashamed who knows who I am." Do we make it clear in life that we belong to Jesus?

Lights, of course, need power to make them work. This comes from the battery of a car, and the lights fail if the contacts are not kept clean. Do we keep clean the contacts we have with God from whom we get our power? These contacts are prayer, love, obedience, the reading of the Bible. It is only through these contacts that Jesus can shine through us.

Romans 1 : 16

9

ESCALATORS

DO you know what an escalator is? It is a moving staircase and you find them in big stores and at stations on the Underground railway. You just step on and are carried up or down without any effort on your part.

How different it is when you want to climb a mountain. Then you have to toil hour after hour until, with a sore back and blistered feet, you eventually get to the top.

Yet there is far more pleasure and satisfaction from climbing the mountain than from travelling on the escalator. There is the wonderful view from the top, the great feeling of peace at the summit, and above all the thrill of knowing that you have done it by your own effort.

Lots of boys and girls wish life was like a moving staircase. When they are at the bottom of the class they wish they could step on to an escalator and get to the top without study and effort. When they first start to learn to play the piano or the violin they would like to become great musicians without spending hour after hour practising scales. But things do not work out that way, and a good thing too.

If life had no challenges to climb, it would be dull and uninteresting. Purpose, courage, perseverance, would have no place. Life would not be grand and exciting and there would be no heroes or heroines.

God made life the way it is, so that we can get satisfaction out of putting real effort into doing something well. Nothing worthwhile is ever achieved without hard work. The easy way is seldom the best way in the long run. God has given us all certain talents and abilities and we can only be happy when we use them to the full. It may be very tempting to step on the escalator, but true character only comes out when we take the trouble to climb the mountain.

This is the secret of being a Christian. To be a follower of Jesus is to be climbing all the way up the mountain of life. There is no magic staircase waiting to whisk us up to the top. The real pleasure of life is when, having put all our effort into the climb, we are able with Jesus' help to stay at the top and share the wonderful peace of the summit.

Matthew 16:24

BUILT TO SCALE

TODAY I want to tell you about a special village I once visited on holiday. It had everything you can think of. There were lovely old-fashioned houses; farms with cows, sheep, pigs, horses and ducks. There was even a lovely old castle. Running through the village was a river with an old mill by its side.

It was a very busy village with a good modern railway, a busy harbour, and even an airport. While we were there we saw a cricket match, a foxhunt and people playing on bowling greens and tennis courts. In the streets were all kinds of shops and inns. It had three churches, and as we passed by we could hear lovely organ music.

I wonder if you have noticed something strange about what I have said so far? A village—with a harbour and an airport and a river and so on? It must have been a very large village. Actually it was very small indeed, with houses only three feet high. It was the model children's village at a place called Beconscot.

What was so wonderful about it was that everything was built to scale—an exact copy of the real thing.

Boys and girls often think they are not important because they are small, but that is not true. What really matters is whether or not they are built to scale, and if they are models of the real thing.

If you want to build a model of anything you make sure that your pattern is the best of its kind. You then find out all you can about it and make your copy as near as possible to the original.

This also applies to life. Each boy and girl is busy building a life, and because of your age it must be a smaller version than an adult, yet built to scale. Very often the example you are following is a grown-up you love and admire, and if you are lucky you may perhaps be successful. Unfortunately, some grown-ups are not the best examples to copy, with the result that the model is not as good as it might be.

Surely the sensible thing is to copy the best example we know, and beyond doubt that means Jesus. We cannot hope to be exact to scale copies of Jesus, but that should not keep us from trying to model our lives on Him. We have all the information we need about Him in the Bible, and if we study His life and teaching He will help us to grow as like Him as is humanly possible.

The Beconscot village is so wonderful because every detail has been carefully copied. Your life too can be wonderful if you do all in your power to copy Jesus in thought, word and deed.

1 *Corinthians* 11 : 1

II

TAPE RECORDERS

HAVE you ever used a tape-recorder? As you know, it is the machine that records whatever you say or sing so that you can play it back and hear your own voice.

What a shock it can be the first time you try it! Your voice seems so different from what you thought it was. If you did not recognize the words you would not believe your own ears. The hard fact is that the recorder tells the truth, and that is really what you sound like to other people.

One good thing about a tape-recorder is that it helps you to correct your mistakes. It tells you where you have gone wrong in your use of words or in your accent. If, when you have been singing, you have taken a breath at the wrong place, this comes out clearly on the recorder, and you will not commit the same fault the next time.

Sometimes at parties a tape-recorder is hidden in the room and later when it is played back all sorts of embarrassing things are heard. Often, things you have said that you did not want others to hear are picked up by the microphone.

I often think of God doing for us what the tape-recorder does to our voice. God sees us as we really are. We may pretend to be different and try to hide our faults and failings from others, and even from ourselves, but God is never deceived. He always knows us better than we know ourselves. He always sees us as we are in our hearts.

God also helps us to find out our mistakes. He has given us the perfect example in Jesus, and when we compare our lives with Him we see our errors. God goes further than that. He not only helps us to see our faults but gives us strength to rectify them. If we really try, Jesus will help us.

Lastly, we must remember that God is always listening to us. Surely this makes us ashamed at many of the things we have said. Some people seem to think that God is only tuned in to our wave-length when we are actually praying to Him. This is not the case. He always hears us and so we ought to try to ensure that He never hears us say things of which we would be ashamed or with which He would be angry.

Always remember that a tape-recorder is a machine that can be switched on and off as we please, but God is always near us day by day.

Luke 16:15

12

ALARMS

ARE you good at waking up in the morning? If you are like me you probably need a good strong alarm to keep you from sleeping in. In Bible times there were no clocks as we know them, but an alarm was sounded on a trumpet. People could sleep soundly knowing that if anything went wrong they would be awakened by the trumpet.

In life, of course, there are many kinds of alarms, not just to waken you but to keep you safe and well. If you carelessly walk on to a road, a car-driver will toot on his horn. When you come to a crossing, the red light will warn you not to cross. If there is something wrong with your body, a pain will give the alarm. All the time we have warnings of the dangers in life.

Each one of us has a built-in alarm. We sometimes call it our conscience. Just at the right time it goes off, and if we listen to it we will keep from saying the nasty word or doing the unkind deed.

I started by talking about an alarm clock, but it will not work unless it is set beforehand. It must be told when to ring, and the clock must always be kept wound up. Our built-in alarm must also be set; our conscience must be kept wound up. It must be shown when to warn us; it must know what is right or wrong, what is good or bad.

This is where the teaching of Jesus comes in. He must be our example. We must set our alarm by Him, so that when we are tempted to think or say or do anything Jesus would not like, our conscience will immediately warn us.

Each time we learn something new about what Jesus said or what Jesus did, we are training our conscience and setting our alarm. The more we learn about Him, the more safely we can journey through life, knowing that as we face temptations and difficulties we will be warned in time to keep us from falling into sin.

But, remember, an alarm is no use unless it is obeyed. There is no point in setting your alarm for eight o'clock in the morning if you are going to turn over and fall asleep again until ten o'clock. So too there is no point in training your conscience unless you intend to obey its warning. Many people know Jesus' teaching but ignore it in their living. Let your built-in alarm, your conscience, not only be trained and set, but make sure you obey its warnings so that you may follow the way of Jesus and serve Him at all times.

Romans 2 : 15

30

13

NEW WINE AND NEW BOTTLES

WHEN we read in the Bible about bottles, we often think of present-day milk bottles or lemonade bottles made of glass. The bottles in the Bible were not like this at all. I am sure you have all seen pictures of Palestine with people carrying bottles made of the skin of a goat. When they are new they are soft and pliable but when they get old they become very hard. It is then that they are likely to burst when filled with water or wine. The safest way is to take new skins for new wine; there is no use just trying to patch the old skins; they will just burst again.

Jesus used two illustrations to tell His message. He spoke of old and new skins and also about patching old garments with new cloth. The new patch may look fine but as soon as it gets wet the new cloth is likely to shrink and tear the stitching apart and so make an even bigger hole.

What was Jesus' message? Simply that we should always try to make our lives new instead of just patching up the old. It is always better to start a new page, or turn over a new leaf, instead of scoring out, blotting, or making alterations on the old sheet on which we have made our mistakes.

You are still young, and you are therefore building a new life. Jesus wants to help you to make something of which you can be proud. Inevitably you will make mistakes. You cannot hope to go through life without leaving marks on your nice clean sheet, but do not try to cover them up or patch them.

Take a new bottle or wine-skin and start afresh. Jesus came to make all things new and He will help you. By just adding patches here and there you leave yourself with a coat that can give way easily in many places but a new coat gives you greater determination to keep it strong and whole.

Each time you go wrong, do not be content with merely correcting your mistake, but start again to make a life which will satisfy Jesus. This is the only kind of life that in the end is really worthwhile.

Matthew 9:17

14

SWORD OF THE SPIRIT

IN Paul's Epistle to the Ephesians we read that "the sword of the spirit is the word of God". Today I want to remind you of three things about swords: they can be used to attack an enemy, or to defend against danger, but in either case they must be sharp or they are of no use. Let us think of Jesus' message as a sword.

It can be used to attack enemies. The enemies in this case are evil, wrong, things that bring unhappiness, sorrow, misery, and sadness. With the help of Jesus, each one of us must attack these things before they can do harm. If we read through history we will find that all truly great men have used the sword of Jesus' teaching to make life better for you and me and all mankind. So many of the things we take for granted have come to us because men attacked great evils in Jesus' name. It was His message that was used to free slaves, to build hospitals, to fight disease, to stop boys and girls from having to work from early morning till late at night. We must use that same sword to attack the evils we meet on the road of life.

It can be used to defend us. We are often tempted to do what is wrong in Jesus' sight. You have all heard of an octopus—a kind of fish with eight long tentacles or arms. In tropical seas, where the octopus lives, swimmers carry a little sword or dagger in a belt, for if they get caught by one of the octopus' arms they have no way of getting free except by cutting it off. Temptations are like the octopus. We cannot get free except by cutting them right out with the sword of Jesus.

But a sword is no use unless it is kept sharp. If we hope to use the sword of Jesus' message, we must keep it sharp in our minds and in our hearts. We must read it and study it every day. It must become part of our daily living, always ready to be used to attack the evils of life and to defend us against life's temptations.

No one can claim to be a Christian unless he carries always with him, sharp and ready, the sword of the message of Jesus.

Ephesians 6:17

15

FEATHERS

WHAT comes to your mind when I mention the word "feather"? A Red Indian chief with his great head-dress? A nice comfortable pillow to rest your head on at night? The kind of pen—a quill-pen—used by our grandfathers before pen-nibs and ball-points were thought of?

Do you think of a very strong feather, like an eagle's wing carrying him high up into the sky; or a soft feather on the mother bird's breast to keep her young ones warm? Is it very long, like that of an ostrich, or tiny like the small feathers on your budgie, or even the kind made up into hats for ladies?

When feathers are mentioned in the Bible they are usually the beautifully-coloured plumes of the peacock, but in Psalm 91 we read: "God shall cover thee with His feathers and under His wings shalt thou trust."

You all know that when a mother bird lays her eggs she sits on them to keep them warm until the chickens are hatched, but she does not leave it there. Until the baby birds are big enough to look after themselves she keeps them safe and warm under her feathers. There they are never afraid, and when any danger approaches they immediately hide beneath her wings.

We are God's children, and the Psalmist tells us that God looks after us in the same way. He covers us with His feathers and under His wings we need never be afraid.

Whatever we have to face in life, God is looking after us. He is standing over us just like a mother bird with her chicks. When danger approaches He is always near us and we can shelter beneath the shadow of His wings.

This does not just apply when we are children. Even when we are old enough to look after ourselves, God is keeping watch over us. In Jesus He has given us His way to walk in and has promised to help us in our journey through life. Jesus said: "Lo, I am with you always." His wings are spread above us and we need never be afraid.

Psalm 91 :4

16

AS PRECIOUS AS GOLD

WOULD you like to own a gold mine? I am sure you are already thinking of all the things you could buy if you had lots of gold. You are thinking how happy you could be if only you had plenty of money to spend.

If you are really unselfish, you are perhaps remembering all the good causes you could help; all the poor folk you know who could do with a little bit extra.

Today there are many people who live their lives with just one purpose in mind; to get the money to buy all the things they would like.

But remember, gold (or money) is not the most important thing in life. You cannot go into a supermarket and buy happiness, or health, or love, or a new life. That is why the Bible tells us there are other things more precious, more important, than gold.

What things? Obeying God; following the example of Jesus; loving our neighbours. These are the most valuable things of all. They may not surround us with television sets, or washing machines, or central heating, or motor cars. They will not help us to keep up with the people next door.

They will, however, bring into our lives happiness

and peace and love. They will also affect the lives of others.

In His Sermon on the Mount, Jesus spoke of the people who are always concerned about the things money can buy: what they can eat and drink, what they can wear.

Then He went on: "But seek ye first the kingdom of God and His righteousness; and all these things shall be added unto you."

First things first. Of course we need money to live— to pay our rent, to buy food, to look after those who are depending on us. To get that money we must work hard and use all our talents. But God must come first and if He does, He will help us to do all other things better.

It would be fun to have a gold mine. It would be nice to be rich. These things, by themselves, cannot bring satisfaction to life. We must concentrate on the really important things in life—the things of God.

"More to be desired are they than gold, yea than much fine gold."

Psalm 19:10

17

MAGNIFYING GLASS

DO you collect stamps? If so, one of your special pieces of equipment will be a magnifying glass. Without it you will be unable to see all the special details that make a stamp so valuable.

There are, of course, many kinds of magnifying glasses. You will all have seen the small one a watchmaker fixes on to his eye to examine the tiny wheels and springs that make a watch keep going.

Or there is the very big one in a lighthouse which sends the beam of light far out to sea.

Large or small, they all serve the same purpose— to enable small things to be made larger so that they can be easily seen.

When we are ill, and the doctor is not sure what is wrong, he takes a sample of our blood, and by using a kind of magnifying glass he can see the tiny germs that are causing our illness. Then he can make us better.

I sometimes think of Jesus' teaching as a magnifying glass. Its shows up the things that are wrong in our lives so that we can do something about them. The things we sometimes cannot see by ourselves, or think of as unimportant, yet which cause harm and unhappiness to us and to others.

Just as the magnifying glass shows up the faults in a precious stamp, or the jeweller's glass tells what is wrong with a hair spring, or the lighthouse warns far-off shipping of dangerous rocks, so the message of Jesus continually reveals the errors in our lives.

There is also a sense in which the Bible tells us we have to play the part of magnifying glasses. In our lives and in our daily living we have to show Jesus' love and kindness and sympathy. We have to make these things large and real so that others cannot help seeing them. Only in this way will they want to share them and so come to Jesus too.

Romans 11:13

18

THE HIGHWAY CODE

DO you all know the Highway Code? It tells us how we should behave on the roads whether we are pedestrians (on foot) or cyclists or drivers.

If we all obeyed the Highway Code there would be far fewer accidents, and fewer people would be injured or killed on our streets. In the Highway Code we find the explanations for all the road signs. Some are to warn us of dangerous bends and difficult crossings, others forbid us to do certain things for our own and others' safety. As Christians who are responsible to God for our own lives and who have a love and concern for others, we all ought to obey the Highway Code.

However, we are all on a journey through life and there is another kind of highway code that is even more important for us. We might call it the Highway Code of Jesus. If we study the Bible we shall find there how we should behave on the road of life.

It too warns us of the dangerous bends we may find and the difficult crossings we may come to. It calls these things temptations, and shows us how, with the help of Jesus, we may safely continue our journey. It too forbids us to do certain things for our own and others' safety. There are, for example, the Ten Commandments, and unless we obey them we are heading straight for trouble.

When some people get behind the wheel of a car they become like demons, having no thought for the welfare of others. When some boys and girls get on a bicycle they become reckless and careless and show off to such an extent that the lives of others are endangered. Some pedestrians blindly cross the street as though they were defying motorists to hit them.

The same is unfortunately true in living. Some people think so much of themselves that they just push all others aside; some live recklessly, not only harming themselves but also those near to them.

If we follow the example of Jesus, if we obey His commandments; if we really love our neighbours, our lives will be different. We will bring happiness to ourselves and to others. We will, in fact, travel safely along the road of life.

It is surely worth while accepting, understanding and obeying Jesus' Highway Code.

Matthew 22:39

19

SETTING SAIL

MOST boys and girls are interested in ships. Those who live in the country look forward to the holidays when they can go to the seaside and play about in boats. Those who live near the sea must often watch the great ships sailing past to their unknown destinations.

In the Bible we find references to all kinds of ships, for example, Noah's wonderful Ark, and the fishing boats so familiar to Jesus, and the bigger ships that took St. Paul to faraway Rome.

Today there are two things I want to say about ships. The first is that ships are no use unless they can move across the water. They may just have oars by which they are pulled slowly along, or sails that catch every wind, or motors that chug merrily round the coast, or great powerful engines propelling the big liners across the oceans. Whatever size they are, they must have some power to move them, otherwise they will just drift aimlessly on to some hidden rocks.

Secondly, they must be steered. It is not enough that they can move; they must be guided to their destination, even if it means bringing in an outside pilot who knows the hidden dangers.

Our lives are like ships. They too must move. We can never get anywhere in life unless we have some power driving us. We may not need to go far or travel very fast, but to move at all we must have a source of power.

The best source of power is Jesus. He keeps us from drifting, from wasting our lives. He gives us the power to travel across the ocean of life to a worthwhile destination.

Our lives must also be steered, otherwise we will perish on the rocks. Who better to guide us than Jesus, who knows all the rocks and dangers and can guide us safely into harbour.

As boys and girls we may travel slowly like a boat with oars; later we may hoist sail and spin more quickly across the waters; then when we grow up to adulthood we may have the power of turbines to tackle any winds or waves. Whatever our age or size, we need the power of Jesus, and need Him too as our Pilot so that we may go His way.

John 6:17

20

THE ROPE OF HAIR

THERE is an old story about a king who wanted to build a new palace and all his subjects loved him so much that each wanted to help. The cost was very great, and all who had money gave whatever they could, from the thousands of pounds of the very rich to the few coppers of the poor. But money was not enough.

So all the men and the boys gave their labour for nothing. The craftsmen used their skills, and the others did the heavy work of labourers, preparing the foundations and carrying all the materials to the site of the new palace.

The roof of the palace was to be built on top of great wooden pillars 50 feet high, and so great trees were cut down, trimmed, then rolled and pushed to their correct position. The difficulty was to erect these massive pillars. There was no rope big enough or strong enough to do the job.

This is where the women and girls came in. They wanted to help but they had no money, nor did they have the strength to do work like the men and the boys. But they all had long hair. So they cut their hair: the grey hair of the old ladies; the long thick tresses of the other women; the golden curls of the girls. Off came their hair and it was twined into a thick rope that stretched for a hundred yards. With this the heavy pillars were lifted into position and so the palace was built.

Jesus does not ask us for our hair, but He does want our hearts. Are we ready to give them to Him as the women and girls were ready to give their hair for their king?

Remember too that a single hair would not have been much use in the story, but when all the hair was put together it was strong enough to lift the heavy pillars.

As individuals there may not seem much we can do, but when we are bound together in Jesus we can do great things.

Matthew 22:37

21

SOMETHING FOR NOTHING

TODAY, everyone seems to want something for nothing. Even boys and girls go about looking for what they can get rather than for what they can give.

There is a story in the Bible which reminds us that

what we get for nothing seldom means very much to us.

King David had been very foolish, and in a state of remorse he decided to build an altar to God. The site he chose was the threshing-floor of a man named Ornan. When Ornan knew what the king wanted, he felt very honoured that part of his ground should be chosen, and he immediately offered the ground to the king for nothing. David refused. He knew he could never find satisfaction in what he was doing unless it had cost him something.

Here is something we all need to learn, boys and girls. There are so many things in life today that we get for nothing, with the result that we do not value them; we just take them for granted.

The boy or girl who has to do errands, or deliver papers, to get the money to buy something he or she specially wants, will appreciate that thing far more than the person who always gets anything he asks for.

But in a very special sense this message has to do with what we give to God. Jesus spoke of the widow's mite being more valuable than the expensive coin tossed in by the rich man. It meant far more because it was a greater sacrifice. It is easy to put a coin into a collection for the poor, but it is far better to spend an hour or two helping the needy.

David said, "I will not offer to God something that cost me nothing." So he paid Ornan the full price for his threshing-floor.

God only wants from us something that is worthwhile. He does not want the offering we think we can spare after we have satisfied all our own needs and desires. We must only offer to Him that which has cost us something—in time, in effort, in sacrifice.

He has given us so much—surely what we return to Him must be of real value to us.

1 *Chronicles* 21 : 18–27

22

SPIDERS FOR LUCK

WOULD you like to collect spiders? I am sure the girls would not, but there is a man in Scotland who does just that. Perhaps it is wrong to say he collects them, but he buys them from all over the country and sells them again.

To understand why, we must go back to just before the battle of Bannockburn when Robert the Bruce led the victorious Scots against the English. The story goes that Bruce was hiding in a cave in despair when he saw a spider suspended from the roof. Trying to make the foundation for its web the spider tried time after time until at last he was successful. This inspired Bruce to keep on trying until he too succeeded.

The man who collects the spiders looks after Bruce's cave and sells them to tourists as good-luck charms. How can a spider bring anyone good or bad luck!

Yet this kind of thing happens everywhere. If you ever visit the Holy Land, you will be pestered by folk selling souvenirs. At every place which had a special significance for Jesus, there is a shrine and a stall displaying souvenirs which are supposed to be the real thing: bits of the rock on which Jesus fed the 5,000; nails from the Cross of Calvary; pieces of wood from the Cross; bits of the stone that was rolled away from the tomb. They are false, of course, yet people still buy them for luck.

How can a nail, or a piece of wood, or a bit of stone, or even a spider, possibly bring good luck or bad luck?

There is only one way to try to have good luck and that is to live your life properly. The best way to do that is to follow Jesus' example and obey His teaching.

When things go right, He will share our happiness. If things go wrong, He will give us the strength and guidance to cope with our problems.

If we trust in Jesus we will not need to depend on good-luck charms or souvenirs.

1 *Timothy* 4:10

23

SWIMMING IN THE DEAD SEA

CAN you swim? This is one thing that all boys and girls should learn to do, especially if they have a swimming-pool near their homes. Even if you cannot swim, there is one place you could go bathing without being in danger of drowning. Do you know where it is? The Dead Sea.

You know where it is, of course. In Palestine, near Jericho. There it is very, very warm, and although the water looks dirty most people go in for a dip. The water feels very strange and whenever you let yourself go you float. You can turn this way and that, lift your knees up to your chin, do all sorts of tricks, even read a paper but you will not sink.

Why? Because the water is six times more salt than the ocean. One explanation for this is that, though the River Jordan flows into the Dead Sea, there is no outlet. Therefore nothing can live in it.

This is true about our lives. Lots of people are quite happy to float about but, unless they have an outlet, a purpose in life, they get nowhere; they do not really live.

If we only receive and never give out we cannot possibly enjoy life to the full. This is also true about love—especially God's love. If we only let it into our hearts and never share it with others, it means nothing to us.

The Good News of Jesus obviously means nothing to us if we try to keep it to ourselves instead of sharing it with others. We can only enjoy it properly when we give it away.

It may be very tempting to float about doing nothing, going nowhere, but that is definitely not living as God intended us to live. Do not let your life be like the Dead Sea. Make sure it really lives by taking in all that is fresh and good, and then have a purpose and an outlet, sharing your gifts with others.

The more you give out, the more you will be able to receive in of God's goodness.

Matthew 19:17

24

GREYFRIARS BOBBIE

HAVE you ever been to Edinburgh, the capital of Scotland? If so you may have seen a statue. Obviously there are many statues in the streets of the city, but I am thinking of a very special one, not of a great man but of a dog. It overlooks the famous churchyard of Greyfriars.

A long time ago, there was an old carter and his dog.

The old man was lonely and his only friend was his dog Bobbie. When he died, only one friend followed his body to its grave—his dog. The people in authority chased the dog away many times, but always it returned ragged, wet, and hungry, to the grave of its master.

A kindly farmer heard the story of Bobbie's devotion and gave the dog a home in the country many miles from Edinburgh. Then one day Bobbie disappeared and some time after it was back again with bleeding, torn paws at the graveside in Greyfriars. So the faithful dog kept up its watch for fourteen years until it was found dead by the graveside.

Now there is an interesting addition to this story. Alongside the churchyard was a row of very poor houses. They were dirty, uncared for and very dark, for even the windows were left dirty. Then there was a change. The children in these houses heard about Bobbie and his faithful watch, and each day they would look out of their windows to see if he was still there. To do this they had to clean the windows. This meant that sun and light came into these old houses and even the lives of the people were affected.

So Greyfriars Bobbie, by his love for his master, brought life and sunshine into the lives of these poor children and their families. By our devotion to our Master, Jesus, we too can bring light and love and sunshine into the hearts and lives of others.

If a small dog could make such a difference, how much more could we if we let Jesus use us.

Romans 8:28

25

A CACTUS GARDEN

TODAY we have our flower service—and how beautiful the flowers all look. The delicate shades and tints, the perfectly formed petals and leaves. No wonder Jesus said about the lilies of the field that "even Solomon in all his glory was not arrayed like one of these".

Most of our flowers today have been grown in hothouses or carefully tended gardens, but even what we call wild flowers, the ones to be found in the meadows and the hedgerows, are equally beautiful and wonderfully formed.

It is therefore natural that we should give thanks to God for all the beauty of His creation in our flower service today.

But I have a garden that does not have beautiful flowers. Instead, they are ugly and prickly. It is a cactus garden. These strange plants normally grow in desert places, and if you were lost in a desert you might even think them beautiful for a very special reason. If you cut them open you will find they contain liquid and many people have been saved from thirst by the cactus.

Let us thank God then, not just for the things that

are beautiful, but also for the things that are ugly yet useful. This is something we sometimes forget to do. We remember only the very nice things in life, and try to forget the things we do not like, but without which life would not be the same.

We are always grateful for sweets but seldom for the nasty-tasting medicine that cures our ills. Both come from God.

We think only of the beautiful trees but often forget to give thanks for the coal which has come from the trees of thousands of years ago.

We give thanks for all our fun and games and our health and strength to enjoy them, but what about thanking God for our schools, and lessons, and studies, that make us strong mentally as well as just physically.

Let us all give thanks to God for all the flowers of life but never forget to be grateful for the cactus as well.

Matthew 6:29

Harvest

26

LEAVE SOME LYING

THE story of the Harvest Festival goes right away back to the Old Testament. There in the Book of Deuteronomy we are told that the firstfruits must be offered to God as a thank-offering. It is sometimes hard for those of us who live in towns and cities to realize how important the harvest is to folk who work on the land. We buy our harvest gifts in the shops or in the markets, but we are in fact saying thanks to God that He has provided all these things for our needs.

One of the important aspects of the harvest in Palestine was that of sharing God's gifts with the less fortunate. Even the oxen were not muzzled as they threshed the grain but were allowed to eat as they worked.

According to Deuteronomy, some must always be left on the ground for the poor and needy. Whether it be grapes or olives or corn—whatever the harvest, the firstfruits go to God and others in need must be given a share.

This is still true today for all who believe in Jesus. We have come to say thanks to God and to share His gifts. The gifts we have brought to this service will be distributed to the sick and the needy. This, however, should not just be done at harvest-time. We think of all the people who are in need throughout the world: the people who live in a state of famine; the great masses of undernourished and underprivileged people in Asia and Africa.

God has supplied all the needs of men, but men have not shared them, so that some are rich and others are poor.

It is the duty of the followers of Jesus to share God's gifts. This applies not only to material things or the things of the harvest. It also applies to God's truth and

God's word. That is why we must continue to send out our missionaries to let other people share with us the joy of knowing and loving Jesus.

Deuteronomy 24:19

27

SHEEP DOGS

HAVE you ever watched Sheep Dog Trials? They are a popular holiday attraction in many parts of the country. They are also a wonderful exhibition of how men and animals can work together as a team.

Sheep dogs, of course, do their normal work across wide areas of hills, but for the trials a special stage is set out. A field is marked out with a small sheep-pen in the centre. The cast includes five sheep, the shepherd and his dog. The trial consists of moving the sheep from one place to another, taking individual sheep away from the others, and finally getting all five sheep into the pen and keeping them there.

Some shepherds keep shouting at their dogs until the dogs get so bewildered they don't know what they are doing. They get to the stage when they cannot depend on the orders of their masters. Some dogs, particularly the young ones, bark so much that the sheep get frightened and either will not move at all or panic in terror. Other dogs become too enthusiastic. They ignore the shepherd and try to do everything on their own. They race about all over the place chasing one sheep and forgetting about the other four.

The winner is usually the team where the shepherd and his dog work as one. Few words are needed—just the occasional whistle. The dog works silently, patiently, always on the alert. It is a wonderful sight.

There is a lesson in this for us. We have the opportunity of working with God. We know we can depend upon Him. We know He will give us clear instructions.

Many of us are too enthusiastic. We rush about making a lot of noise and bringing attention to our good works. But so often we just frighten people away from Jesus. Others try to do things on their own. They don't wait for instructions. They think they know best. But without God we can do nothing.

The true Christian is one with God. With Christ in his heart he knows exactly what God wants. He does it quietly. He is always on the alert for God's guidance.

It is a wonderful sight to see the shepherd and his dog working in complete understanding. It is a wonderful experience for us to work in complete understanding with God.

John 15:5

28

WISE AS AN OWL

WE speak of the "wise old owl". I wonder why? In the Bible it is not looked upon as a friendly bird. It is always out at night when it is dark. Wicked men are called owls because they hate the light. Even its appearance is one of cruelty, with its fierce beak and its horrible claws.

Yet, despite these things, most of us have a soft spot for the owl. We are ready to overlook its faults and think only of its good points. What are they?

All day the owl perches quietly, apparently sleeping. This gives him the appearance of a wise old man who is deep in thought. He looks so serious that you feel you could only disturb him if you had something very important to ask him. All the time, however, you know that he is on the alert, ever watchful behind those half-closed eyes.

We should try to be more like the owl. Instead of always wanting to be heard, to get our word in before everyone else, we ought to sit quiet and listen. Then, when we do speak, others will pay attention because they will know we have something worthwhile to say.

We should also be ever-watchful. Always on the alert. Temptations come upon us so quickly in life that unless we are ready we shall fall into them. If we are caught unawares, we will do things that are wrong, and say things that hurt others and make them unhappy. If, however, we are on our guard and ready to resist these temptations, God will help us.

To follow Jesus we must try to be like the owl. Not the cruel hard one of the Bible, but the "wise old owl" we have come to know. Remembering how to keep quiet, only speaking when we have something worthwhile to say, and always on the alert to serve Jesus and ready to do His will.

Psalm 102 : 6

29

ALADDIN'S LAMP

I AM sure you all know the story of Aladdin and his wonderful Lamp. By rubbing the Lamp he could get whatever he wanted. If you had Aladdin's Lamp, and, by rubbing it, could get one wish realized—what would you wish for?

Money? Why waste a wish when you can get money if you are prepared to work hard enough to make it? Remember, money cannot buy everything. For example, it cannot buy you good health if you are ill.

A nice house; clothes, etc? Of course money could buy these, but again money is not everything.

Health? I have already pointed out that money cannot buy good health, yet is something we all desire, Even good health, however, is not enough. There are many healthy people who clearly have something missing in their lives.

Happiness? Many people think happiness comes from just playing games and having a good time, but this is wrong. Happiness comes from living a good life, thinking not just of ourselves but of others.

I don't think Aladdin's Lamp could bring happiness, but I can tell you where to get it. In the Bible!

The Bible tells us how to live, and gives us the example of Jesus to prove it. There is no point in just reading about that example. We must try to follow it.

Too many people today are trying to get what they want from Aladdin's Lamp, instead of putting some effort into living a good life. They want money—so they try the football pools and gambling, instead of working hard to earn it. They want health—yet they ruin their bodies with drugs and alcohol. They want happiness—and are always searching for it for themselves instead of thinking about others.

Jesus said, "Seek ye first the Kingdom of God . . . and all these others shall be added unto you." What did he mean? Simply that, if we follow the example of Jesus, we will make the best use of our money; we will take care of our bodies; and we will find happiness in helping others.

Matthew 6:33

30

RUBBING OUT MISTAKES

DO you ever make mistakes at school? I am sure that even those of you who are very clever sometimes slip up. If so, you will realize that it is not always easy to rub out the errors.

When you are using the blackboard and chalk, you can usually make alterations without them being noticed. You just rub out the mistake with a duster and put in the correct answer.

If you are using pencil and paper, a good soft rubber will help you, though sometimes even this leaves a slight mark which can be seen by others.

With pen and ink it becomes much harder. A hard rubber alters the surface of the paper so that when you put in the right answer the ink smudges. Even if you have some of the special liquid that dissolves the ink, it is still possible to see where the alteration was made.

The mistakes we make in life are just as difficult to hide. The wrongs we do when we are very young can, like the chalk marks on the blackboard, be wiped out and replaced by the things that are right.

When we make these same errors again, however, they are not so easily rubbed out. The marks become much deeper. Like pencil on paper, the mistakes can be rectified but the impressions still remain.

As we grow older we move from the pencil stage to that of the pen and ink. The wrongs that we do cannot be hidden. The surface of our lives becomes smudged for everyone to see.

Yet as Christians we have an answer. Jesus has promised us forgiveness, if we but ask Him. This does not mean that we forget our mistakes, otherwise we would keep on making them again and again. It does mean that Jesus, by His forgiveness, will help us to remove the marks of our sins so that we can show to the world a life that is clean, and true, and attractive.

1 *John* 1 : 9

31

JELLYFISH

HAVE you ever tried to catch jellyfish at the seaside? If not, I would warn you that they can have some very nasty side-effects. At least you know what they look like—just blobs of stuff like table-jellies drifting with the tide. They have no backbone. They just drift about as though they were saying, "Why waste energy trying to swim? I'm quite happy as I am."

Often we see them lying dead on the rocks and we feel

a bit sorry for them. "Poor things, they have been left high and dry by the tide." Nonsense! It is just that they are so lazy, and enjoy just lying in the sun, that they make no effort to get into the water. The result is that they shrivel up and die.

Many folk are content to drift along in life, making no effort to live. Like the jellyfish, they have no backbone. They are quite content to let the tide of life carry them here and there. They are so ready to lie in the sun doing nothing that eventually they just shrivel up and die as human beings.

Anyone who follows Jesus knows this to be wrong. He did not offer us a nice easy-going life without effort on our part. He told us that life would be hard, demanding all our strength and determination, but in the effort we would find joy and happiness.

Nothing in life is worthwhile if it comes too easily. The great athlete must keep on training. The great musician must practise day after day. The great professor must study and study and study.

To make a success of life we must always be putting effort into our living. We cannot sit back and wait for success to come to us.

To be a jellyfish is to be a failure. We must constantly swim against the tide if we are to avoid temptation and sin.

Matthew 16:24

32

LIGHT AND POWER

DO you live in an old house? If so, you have probably had an electrician in doing something to the wires. Not so long ago it was enough to have an electric light system, but with washing machines, spin-driers, and electric fires, it is necessary to have power plugs as well.

I am not an electrician—all I can do is change a bulb or mend a fuse—but what the electrician does is fairly straightforward.

First, he goes to the main switchboard and puts in a new switch and fusebox. From this he leads a cable, usually stronger than the light cable, to the place where the washing machine or the refrigerator is going to sit. There he fits a new socket and switch. When this is done, he plugs in the new equipment, and it works! This all sounds very simple, if you know how to do it; and that is why we leave it to the expert—the electrician.

I think we can learn a lot of lessons from this simple job of the electrician's.

In life today we need both light and power. Jesus said, "I am the Light." His Light guides us through life and shows us God's way, but we need God's Power to follow the example of Jesus, to do His will. We need both the Light and the Power.

LIGHT AND POWER

The fuse is there for a special purpose. Whenever anything goes wrong the fuse breaks and avoids more serious damage. It breaks the tension.

So too in life there are fuses to break the tension. There are tears which come in times of sadness; in the midst of problems we see the funny side of the situation. And so the tension is eased to keep us from having a nervous breakdown.

The cable is essential. The electric power must be carried along wires from one point to another. If these wires or cables are not strong enough they will break and the supply of power will stop. So too we are God's cables. He uses us to do His will today. Through us He gives help and power to others. If we snap, or are too weak, or get rubbed and frayed, we are no longer of use to God. It is therefore our duty to keep ourselves in a fit condition to be used by God.

Finally, there must be a switch. The cable, the fuse, the electric iron, or the washing machine, are of no use unless the power is switched on. They may all be in perfect working order but helpless without the switch.

We, too, may be ready and in good working order to serve God, but until the power is switched on we are helpless.

How do we switch on God's power? There is only one way and that is through prayer. Prayer is the switch that sends God's power into our lives and through us into the lives of others. Without prayer we can do nothing in His Name.

John 8:12

33

HAVE YOU A ROAD MAP?

HOW do you find your way from one place to another? You can ask a policeman. Of course, that is all right in town, but it is not so easy in the country. The best way is to have a map. Nowadays maps not only tell you how to get from one place to another, but they also give you interesting information about the district—points of historical interest like old castles and battlefields; when the shops close for their half-day; whether it is hill country or farming land.

Most important, especially if you are motoring, modern maps tell you all about the kind of roads you will be using.

Throughout the country there are great motorways along which you can travel with comfort at high speeds. Then there are the main roads, not so straight as the motorways and with more side-roads and junctions. "B" roads are fairly good, but have many bends and twists and call for more careful driving. On these, however, you are likely to see more of the countryside and wild-life.

Some roads are very bad. They have dangerous corners and very steep hills. Their surfaces are very rough. In places there is only room for one car, and special passing places are provided. It is very often on these roads that the most beautiful scenery can be enjoyed, but unfortunately the person who is driving is unable to enjoy it.

A good road map tells you all these things, and so enables you to get quickly from one place to another, or to travel more leisurely and enjoy the countryside.

There is a good road map for the journey of life. It is the Bible. It shows you how to get the most out of your journey. It warns you against the dangers you will encounter. It describes what you will see as you go along and helps you to appreciate the experiences of life. It is important that you young people, as you set out on your journey, should study it well.

Don't forget, though, that the road map is of little use unless you travel. You must set out on your journey before it can be of much help.

The Bible, by itself, will not take you through life. You must first make up your mind where you want to go. You must decide that you want to travel along God's way and then the Bible will help you to reach your destination.

John 14:6

34

SHINING FOR JESUS

IF it is getting dark and you still have homework to do, what do you do? You switch on the light. It is all so simple that we take electricity for granted.

Most houses today use electric lamps, though in some there may still be gas lamps, and in very remote places paraffin lamps. In Bible times, they used oil lamps in which they floated pieces of rag to burn and give light. In comparison with our powerful lights today, these primitive lamps only gave out a tiny flicker; yet they were welcomed because they dispelled some of the darkness.

We often sing the children's hymn, "Jesus bids us shine." It tells us that Jesus wants us to be His lamps, each shining in his own small corner. How can we do that?

When people are sad, we talk about them being in darkness, and when we cheer them up we bring light to their hearts. You can shine your lamp into other people's lives by making them happy; by helping them as best you can; by keeping from doing things that will annoy them or give them trouble.

In most of the big cities there is one day in the year when all the university students dress up in fancy dress and go out on to the streets to collect for charities. In the evening they go round the main streets in a procession of lorries and each student carries a torch. In the darkness, one single torch would not make much difference, but hundreds of torches, all carried together, make a great light.

You may not think you can do much for Jesus—just one "little candle burning in the night", but if we all try to be Jesus' lamps, if we all try to bring a little light and love and happiness into the world, we can chase away the darkness.

Because we are very young, our lamp may just have the glow of the oil lamp of the Bible, but as we grow older it will grow and grow in power until it sheds the powerful light of the electric bulb. The important thing is to keep it shining bright to the best of our ability.

"So let us shine, you in your small corner and I in mine."

Matthew 5 : 16

35

WHITE AS IVORY

HAVE you any ivory in the house? No? Think again. Have you a piano? If so, the white keys are probably made of ivory. Or I am sure you have some ornaments or carvings made by natives of India or Africa from ivory. Ivory, of course, comes from the tusks of elephants, and in the past many elephants have been slaughtered so that the tusk collectors could sell the ivory.

Why is it so important? For two reasons. First, it is easily carved. That is why so many of the world's most beautiful carvings come from the plain tusks of elephants, so skilfully and patiently made by the natives with no other tools than a very sharp knife. Secondly, ivory is important because it keeps its whiteness for a very long time.

These two reasons have a bearing on our lives. We may think we are just plain and ordinary, and have little to offer. Yet with skill and patience something beautiful may be made of us. If only we let Jesus touch our lives, He will make us what He wants us to be, someone worthwhile. After all, if we were important enough for Jesus to die for us, surely we are important enough in His sight to let Him mould us as He will.

By ourselves we may not be able to make much of our lives but in the hands of Jesus great things are possible for all of us.

I said that ivory is important because it does not easily become yellow or stained. Each one of us would like to keep our life fresh and bright. If left to ourselves we become soiled by the evils of life. When we give way to temptations, when we think and say and do things that are wrong, when we blindly just do what others are doing, our lives become stained.

Yet Jesus can help us. If we ask Him, if we try to

follow Him, we can remain as white and unstained as the finest ivory.

Ivory is important because it is easily carved and keeps its whiteness. In the hands of Jesus we can be moulded for good and retain our whiteness and purity.

Matthew 7 : 7

36

JUMBLE SALES

I AM sure you have all been to a jumble sale. There you discover all sorts of queer things; things that are old-fashioned or out-of-date; things that are still useful but are no longer wanted by their owners.

Before a jumble sale people clear out their attics, get rid of the stuff they do not want. Perhaps they have bought a nice new suite of furniture that is very modern and makes some of the older items look out of place. Ornaments that were once attractive now just seem to gather dust. Occasionally things like wirelesses or carpet sweepers are thrown out because they no longer work. It takes very little to repair them but their old owners just cannot be bothered. All these things can be found at a jumble sale.

We need to be spring-cleaned now and then. We must get rid of things that spoil our appearance, like bad temper and nastiness. We must clear out the things that just gather dirt, such as laziness and apathy. We must do away with the things that do not work, like pride and selfishness.

Just as with our homes, we must make our hearts neat and clean. But here lies a danger. Having got rid of the things we do not want we must put other things in their place. Jesus told a story about what happens when we clean out the bad things from our hearts and leave them empty. The bad things come back worse than ever.

Remember, however, not to throw things out just because they are old. Many old things are neither old-fashioned nor out-of-date. The Bible is old but its meaning is still the same. The story of Jesus goes back for 2,000 years but still has an important message for us today. We need to hold on to the good things even though they may be old.

When we have cleaned out our hearts, let us ask Jesus to come in; then they will be kept new and bright.

The things we clean out of our homes may still find a buyer at a jumble sale. The things we clean out of our hearts are no use to anyone and must be destroyed.

Matthew 12:43

37

KEEPING A DIARY

DO you keep a diary? Most diaries contain lots of useful information about the stages of the moon, and Bank holidays, and lighting-up times, and so on. Sometimes there are special diaries for special people such as Scouts, Guides, gardeners or motorists. These of course, have special hints for those who are interested.

The really important pages are the ones inside for each separate day. If you are a busy person, you need a diary to remind you about your engagements; otherwise you might forget to turn up at a meeting or a function.

Diaries are also important as a record of what has passed. It can be good fun looking through an old diary to remind yourself where you went or whom you met.

Real diaries, however, are not just engagement records. They are filled up each day with notes of all that happened, where you went, what you thought. These are the diaries that become famous, like the Diary of Samuel Pepys. Through such diaries future generations can get a true picture of what happened in our time. If you become famous, the diary you are keeping just now may become a best-seller.

If you want to keep a diary like that, you must write it up each night. You must also be very honest about it.

There is no point in just putting in the good things. Unless everything goes in, your diary is useless.

It would be good for us all to keep such a diary. It would encourage us when we had done well. It would be a constant reminder to us when we had gone wrong. Knowing that we had to put down in black and white our faults as well as our successes would help us to be constantly trying to do the best we could.

As one of our New Year resolutions let us try to keep a diary that we need not be afraid of anyone reading. Above all, let it be one that we would not be ashamed of Jesus reading. The simple way to assure this is by trying at all times to live as Jesus wants us to live.

Psalm 139:23

38

"L" FOR LEARNER

WHY do some cars carry an L-plate? Because the driver is only learning and has not yet passed his test.

The L-plate serves two purposes. It is a warning to other drivers that the learner is not yet experienced and may do something wrong. It is also a request to experienced drivers to have patience and understanding for the learner.

"L" FOR LEARNER

To do anything worthwhile we must take the trouble to learn. To learn to play the piano, you must first master the scales. To become a dancer, you start with simple steps. Before you can read, you must know the alphabet. In every subject at school, you start with the simple things, and move on gradually to the more difficult stages. Whatever you do, you must take the trouble to learn.

"L" also stands for "LIVE", and you certainly need to learn how to do that too. To live you must work, and that demands certain training. To live you must have time to play and whatever your sport or hobby it calls for practice. To live properly means more than just work and play. It includes how to get on with other people; to know what things are really important; to be able to tell the difference between right and wrong.

All these things must be learnt. Where do we get our information? From the Bible, from Sunday School. These are the things religion is about. These are what Jesus came to teach us.

To learn any subject we must turn to a good teacher. To learn how to live we can all turn to the best teacher of all, Jesus himself.

As I said before, when you are learning to drive a car you have an L-plate to warn of your inexperience and to ask understanding from other drivers.

In learning to live, your age is your L-plate. Because you are young, others are ready to help when you make a mistake and are willing to treat you with under-standing. They too have had to learn to live and they too know that the example of Jesus is the best guide through life.

Ephesians 6:1

39

BRITISH MUSEUM

HAVE you ever visited the British Museum? Perhaps you have never been to London, but if not, you will have been in other museums which tell the same story. It is the story of the history of mankind told in pottery, silver, carvings, some well over 2,000 years old.

We think our modern age is wonderful. Man has landed on the moon. We can travel at fantastic speeds. We have amazing machines, computers, that can make calculations far quicker than men can work things out on paper. We are very proud of our age and all its achievements. When we are thinking how clever we are it does us good to visit some old museum.

There we will see pots and ornaments with beautiful decorations. Silver work with intricate designs. Carvings that have obviously been executed by dedicated craftsmen. Yet all done by hand with only the most primitive tools. Yes, these folk of long ago were also very, very clever people.

Of course, they did not have television, or motor cars, or electric light, or refrigerators or washing machines. Nor did they have the evil things of our day, such as hydrogen bombs, and poison gases, and betting shops. They made the most of the things they had, so do not let us look down on them as though they were something inferior to our age.

One thing, however, they did not have. Something that we so often just take for granted and therefore do not cherish. They did not have the message of Jesus. They lived before His time.

We are so lucky! We may not be better craftsmen. But at least we have the teaching of Jesus to help us to make the best use of all the discoveries of man. All the wonderful achievements of our age will mean nothing to us unless we use them in God's service.

Yes, we are lucky—if we use God's gifts in the way Jesus has shown us and share them with our fellow-men.

1 *Peter* 4:10

40

AEROPLANES OR GLIDERS?

ARE you an aeroplane or a glider? That may sound a silly question until you think of the difference between the two.

DON'T FEED THE PONIES

If you have ever visited an airport, you will know what a bustling, busy place it is. Planes landing one after another from all parts of the world. Others taking off for strange, unknown destinations. Passengers hurrying to and fro. Luggage being checked in or out. Machines being checked and refuelled. Everywhere there is great activity, yet all know what they are doing and where they are going.

Sometimes, however, when you look up into the sky you see what looks like an aeroplane—but there is no noise. No jet-engine with its deafening roar. No vapour trail. What you are watching is a glider soaring silently through the clouds. It started its flight by being towed, like a kite, and once in the air it depends on the wind, air currents and the skill of the pilot.

Here is the difference between the aeroplane and the glider. One has a powerful engine to take it where it has to go. The other is at the mercy of wind and air—really going nowhere.

People are sometimes like gliders. Some sail along, seemingly enjoying life but in fact getting nowhere. They have no source of power driving them to their goal.

Christians are different. Jesus gives them power to go where they have to go. He gives them meaning and purpose in living.

This makes all the difference in the world. Now is the time to make up your mind whether you want to go through life as an aeroplane or a glider. If you want your life to be a success you must ask Jesus to give you His power to carry you to your goal. Ask for His strength to follow His example, instead of just drifting aimlessly at the mercy of the wind.

Matthew 28:19

41

REINDEER

HAVE you ever seen reindeer? I don't just mean drawings of reindeer pulling Santa Claus' sledge— I mean real, live reindeer. You are probably thinking— how could you, when you have never been to Lapland where they come from. Up in the Scottish Highlands, at a place called Glen More, there is a real live herd of reindeer.

Looking after the herd are Laplanders, dressed in their national, colourful costume. Most folk would say this is just a tourist attraction and this, of course, is true enough. All through the summer, thousands of tourists visit the reindeer herd, and most of them try to get photographs of the herdsmen in their traditional dress.

I like to think that this serves another purpose. The reindeer are settling in nicely to the Scottish scenery but I am sure the sight of the Laplanders makes them feel at home. The strange costume is something they recognize.

It is good for us, wherever we go, to have things we can immediately recognize. Things that help us to live the right way. Things that encourage us to uphold good traditions.

One of the reasons why we bring you to worship or to Sunday school is to teach you about Jesus and His Way. We want you to get to know the Bible right from an early age so that you will always be familiar with it.

Then, when you go out into life where many things will be strange to you, there will always be something you can recognize. When you are in the company of people who have no faith you will have something to hold on to. When you are facing difficult problems you will be able to draw on the guidance of Jesus' message. Always you will have in your heart a reminder of what is good and right.

The colourful Laplander helps the reindeer to feel at home, even in Scotland. The presence of another Christian helps us to feel at home wherever we may go in the world.

John 5:39

42

PASSPORTS

HAVE you ever been abroad? Some of you may have gone to the Continent with school parties. Others may have gone for a holiday to Majorca or even America. It is fairly certain that most of you by the time you have grown up will at least have paid a short visit to some foreign country. If so, you will need a passport.

A passport is a piece of paper which proves that you are a citizen of Britain. It is a very important document. Without it you cannot travel from one country to another. To have a passport is a great privilege—it also carries a great obligation.

The privilege is to have the strength of Britain behind you. If you are in trouble abroad the representatives of our country are there to help you. When you are in a strange land your British passport assures you of the friendship of other Britons and the respect of other nations.

But there is also an obligation in carrying a British passport. You become a representative of Britain. You must therefore set a good example. Other people will judge Britain by the way you behave. You can either uphold Britain or you can let your country down.

Being a member of an organization like the Scouts or the Guides is also a kind of passport. By wearing your badge you will be recognized by others. You will be able to make friends. Others will know you have certain standards you will uphold. By doing wrong, of course, you will let your organization down.

Being a Christian is the best passport of all. It will help you to find friends in all countries, where even though the languages and customs may be different, you have one thing in common—love of Jesus. With His passport you can know that wherever you go you will have His backing.

But the Christian passport also carries a responsibility and an obligation. You must always set the example of a Christian. Wherever you are, you must always ensure that you neither say nor do anything that may make Jesus ashamed that you carry His passport.

I John I : 7

43

FISH SAUSAGES

HAVE you ever tasted fish sausages? No, I haven't made a mistake. I did not mean fish *and* sausages. I meant fish sausages; sausages made with fish instead of meat. Or fish chips—again I have not left out the word "and". I am talking about chips that look and taste like ordinary chips but are made with fish. Or meat roll that is really fish.

These are the things scientists are working on at a fish research station in Scotland and we may soon be able to buy them in the shops. As you know, fish is cheaper and more plentiful than meat and sometimes catches are so big that many of the fish cannot be sold. It was because of this that the scientists decided to use fish for other kinds of food. After many, many experiments they are now able to produce fish sausages, fish chips and fish meat rolls. The results have been exceptionally good and it is hard to tell the difference between the fish products and the real thing.

The real problem lies in the name. Are they fish or are they sausages? People will find it hard to believe that they are both. It shows that you cannot always depend on a name.

We see this in many different ways. When we think of the village blacksmith, we picture him shoeing horses, but now he is an agricultural engineer. The saddler still works with leather but seldom makes saddles. The shoemaker only repairs shoes, he does not make them.

No, you cannot always depend on a name, but one name that never changes is a Christian. It should always mean the same. Wherever you may go, whatever language is spoken, whichever age it may be, a Christian is always a person who follows Jesus.

He is someone who is trying to do what Jesus wants him to do. He is always trying to help others in Jesus' name. He is proud to bear the name of Christ—to be Christ's man. This is a name that never changes.

Romans 1 : 16

44

DON'T WASTE WATER

EVERY summer, notices saying "Don't Waste Water" appear in different parts of the country. For those of us who so often complain about our wet weather, such notices don't seem to make sense. When we think of the snows and the floods during the winter, it seems a bit silly to bother about wasting a little water during the short time there is a hot spell in the summer.

Of course, we are wrong. We use so much water nowadays that it is impossible to store enough to cover all our needs during very dry spells. Our trouble is that we do not value water highly enough. It is too cheap. We just turn on the tap and the water is always there. If we lived in other parts of the world, we would cherish our water supply and be a bit more grateful. In desert places a drop of water can make the difference between life and death.

There is a thrilling story in the Bible about a cup of water. David was fighting the Philistines, and was camped on the side of a hill overlooking Bethlehem, which was occupied by the enemy. As he looked across the valley, he longed for a drink of water from the well at Bethlehem. Unknown to him, three of his leading men decided that they would satisfy the king's desire. Risking their lives they made their way through the enemy lines and brought a cup of the precious water to the king.

David was so touched by their action, and felt the water was so precious that he refused to drink it and poured it out to God. We may feel that was a strange thing to do, but David felt it was the right action.

We do not need to risk our lives to get a drink of water—we just turn on the tap and it is there. But let us always remember that without water we would die. Like so many other things we take for granted, God has supplied it for our need. Though it costs us so little, we must treat it as a gift from God and use it wisely. Above all, we must never fail to thank God for it.

2 Samuel 23:15

45

NAILS

HAVE you ever wondered what we would do without nails? We cannot look around us without seeing them everywhere, keeping things together. Toys and furniture, picture frames and boxes, kennels and skyscrapers—all have nails of all shapes and sizes. Yet if we see a nail lying on the ground we say, "Oh, it's only a nail." Nails are so very ordinary, yet they are also very important. There is a famous poem which tells the story of a missing nail—it was in a horse-shoe, and because the nail was missing, the shoe was lost, the horse fell, and its rider was killed. "For want of a nail, a man was lost."

If a nail comes out, or is lost, it can cause a great deal of damage and harm. The most expensive piece of machinery may come to bits and be destroyed for want of a nail.

It may be just an ordinary nail but it serves an important purpose. We too may think we are just ordinary and unimportant, but in God's sight we are important. Great work and great effort may come to pieces and be wasted if we do not play our part.

Some nails, of course, are very important, depending what they are used for. At Easter time we think especially of the nails used to fasten Jesus to the Cross of Calvary. Before that day they may have been very ordinary nails but they were used for a very extraordinary purpose.

When we talk of the nails used to fasten Jesus to the Cross, we are not only talking about the actual small pieces of metal. We think of the other things which caused Jesus to be crucified.

Envy, greed, selfishness, pride—these were the sins which caused men to crucify Him, therefore we sometimes call them the nails that fastened Him to the Cross.

These are the very nails we can have in our own hearts. Because of them Jesus died, and we must try to rid ourselves of them. It is not always easy, but, because Jesus is risen and alive, He will help us if only we ask.

Nails are ordinary things, yet if used for the right purpose they can play an important part in life. We too may be ordinary, but in God's hands we have an important function to fulfil.

Isaiah 22 : 23

46

THE CHEAT

THERE is an old, old story of a rich man who wanted to help one of his neighbours who was a carpenter or builder. The carpenter was unemployed and was finding it difficult to feed his family, so the rich man asked him to build him a house. The rich man had to go away from home on business, so he left the carpenter to get on with the job by himself.

When the carpenter was left to himself he decided he would cheat the rich man. He did not waste much time on the foundations, which would not be seen when the house was built. He used the cheapest materials he could find. He painted over cracks, and camouflaged bad workmanship. Although it looked all right from outside, the house he built was just a ramshackle building.

Eventually the rich man returned home and the carpenter handed over the house.

"Thank you", said the rich man. "Here are the deeds and the key. The house is yours."

And so the carpenter had robbed himself by cheating his employer.

Boys and girls, as we go through life we find that we reap what we sow. We are each building today the house we must live in tomorrow.

Our character is the house we build for ourselves. If we construct it of shoddy materials, if we ignore the foundations, if we try to whitewash the cracks and camouflage the weaknesses, in the end we ourselves must suffer.

We can build a castle or a slum, a palace or a pigsty—but we must live in it.

This is why it is so important that right from the beginning we get the help of the great builder—Jesus. God has been called the Great Architect of the Universe. We may do the labouring, we can help with the building, but we need the advice, the guidance of God in making our body, our house, our life a palace and not a shack. If we put our best efforts into it, God will bless our handiwork.

1 *Corinthians* 3:10

47

PARCHMENT

I AM sure you have all read in the Gospels how Jesus went into the synagogue (the church building of His day) and read a passage from Scripture. Have you ever wondered what He read from? It was a parchment or scroll written in Hebrew, the language of the Jews.

Parchment was a kind of skin used for writing on before paper was invented, but it was also the name given to books and letters in Bible times.

If you have seen Fred Flintstone on TV, you will know that his letters and newspapers are slabs of stone on which letters are cut out with a hammer and chisel. This was the earliest form of writing. Then skins were used. Later there was a kind of grass or reeds until paper was invented, and books as we know them today were printed.

Because parchment skins were easily cracked or broken they could not be folded and made into pages like the books we have today. They therefore had to be rolled very carefully, and this was called a scroll. The language was that of the people of the time— Hebrew. At each service in the synagogue a little was unrolled, and the passage unfolded was the one used that day—the passage Jesus read.

The wonderful thing is that the same message Jesus read in the synagogue nearly two thousand years ago is still available for us to read today in our Bible. What Jesus read was from what we call the Old Testament—which tells us about the time before Jesus. To this, were added the Gospels, telling us the Good News about Jesus—His life and teaching—and also the story of the early church, which together make the New Testament.

And so, whether it be a message chipped on stone like the Flintstones, or written by hand on parchment scrolls as in Old Testament times, or printed in a book like our present Bible; whether it be written in Hebrew, the language of the Jews, or in Greek as was the New Testament, or in modern English as we have it now; the Bible is still God's Book and God's Word.

We must therefore read it, not just on Sundays but every day. We must try to understand its message. We must follow its teaching day by day.

Luke 4:16

48

WHITER THAN WHITE

DO you ever get tired of reading the soap-powder advertisements that are pushed through your letter-box? Each manufacturer claims that his soap-powder (or detergent, as it is sometimes called) is better than all the others. Obviously they cannot all be right.

However, if you read the advertisements carefully, you will find that they fall into two groups. One group emphasizes how they get rid of all the stains and make the washing look like new. The other group tell you they add extra whiteness—the whiter-than-white powders. The difference between these two groups is interesting and tells us something about life itself.

Many people today are like the stain-remover group. They want to live decent, respectable lives, and are therefore always trying to remove the faults in their lives. They are sorry for their sins and their weaknesses and genuinely try to eradicate their mistakes. They are ready to obey all the rules and the regulations and would not deliberately hurt or offend others.

But is that enough? The Pharisees, in Bible times, were like that. They obeyed a very strict code of conduct. They kept very rigidly to the law of Moses and went out of their way to keep the Commandments. Yet Jesus condemned them. Why? Because they were living negative lives. All they were concerned about was removing the stains and living respectable lives. They were the stain-remover group.

Jesus made it clear that there was more to life than just obeying the laws. It was not enough to remain respectable and law-abiding. We must try to make life better. We must go out of our way to help others. We must live positively, always seeking opportunities of doing more and being better.

It is not enough just to remove the stains, we must try to make our lives whiter than white. Anyone can be good and respectable, but the Christian must do more. According to Jesus he must go the extra mile, he must give his coat *and* his cloak. He must never be satisfied with just keeping the law but must do even better than the law demands.

Boys and girls, do not be content to remain in the stain-remover group. Join the whiter-than-whites and so live active, positive Christian lives.

Isaiah 1 : 18

49

BUTTER OR MARGARINE?

DO you prefer butter to margarine? I don't suppose you are ever asked that question because you just take what mummy gives you. I can remember the time when people had little choice. Real farm butter was a special treat, but in the big cities where there was a lot of poverty many people could not afford to buy butter and had to make do with margarine which was cheaper.

Today, things are different and most people can make a choice. Butter, of course, is made mainly with milk, whereas margarine is made from animal and vegetable fats. In the old days everyone thought butter was far better for you, but now there are many who argue that margarine is the better. I am not taking sides in that argument, so I won't get into trouble with one side or the other. What I am interested in is the answer we often hear given in the TV advertisements: "I couldn't tell the difference."

This is the kind of answer we get so often today—whether it be about butter or margarine, or right or wrong. So many people just cannot tell the difference.

There are many things accepted as normal that would not have been tolerated before. People do things and say things without stopping to ask if they are right or wrong. Instead of taking the trouble to examine the facts on both sides, they just blindly follow the example of others. Life cannot go on that way. We must make choices.

It is not good enough just to follow the crowd and then say: "I couldn't tell the difference."

This is why we are encouraging you to read your Bible and study the teaching of Jesus. It is to help you make the right choices in life. I am not thinking of trivial things like choosing between butter or margarine, but the important things about right or wrong.

Sometimes it is not easy. It may be difficult to choose between two courses of action which is the better, but as Christians we always have help in making our decisions. Would Jesus do that? Would this help or hurt other people? Is this or that just the easy way out? Is this God's way for me? All these questions help us to make the right choice.

If we know the teaching of Jesus. If we are trying to follow His example. If we are putting ourselves in God's hands, then He will guide us in all our decisions.

Unlike the woman in the advertisement, we will be able to tell the difference, and choose what is right.

Joshua 24:15

50

DANDELIONS

I AM sure we all have a soft spot for dandelions. When we see their bright yellow heads, we know that winter is over and summer will soon be with us. Even when the skies are cloudy we have a burst of sunshine in the dandelion patch.

Not everyone, of course, likes the dandelion. When the gardener sees one in his rose-bed he gets annoyed. He knows that this simple flower, or weed, has roots far down in the earth and just cutting off the flower will not solve his problem.

When we talk of the dandelion as a flower, we are not strictly correct, for each golden head is really a cluster of little flowers, each with five tiny petals surrounding the dandelion seed. When the seed is ripe, and the petals fall off, we have the tiny parachutes that children blow into the air to tell the time.

DANDELIONS

One of the great disappointments for children is that the dandelion cannot be tamed. You cannot cut the flower, put it into water and hope it will continue to live. Whenever you take it from the ground it will wilt and die.

The dandelion is not only a touch of sunshine but for centuries has been looked upon as a medicine. Some experts claim it is one of the bitter herbs talked about in the Bible. Even today many people use the dandelion to cure illnesses or as a tasty salad.

So however we look at it—as a menace in the rose garden, or as growing sunshine to children, or as a tasty delicacy to the vegetarians—the humble dandelion is the work of God. It has also something to tell us about life.

We obviously cannot please everyone as we journey through life. What is a touch of sunshine to one is a weed to another. We can therefore only try to do our best, remembering that it is God we must please, not men. He created the dandelion and the rose.

Remember, too, that the dandelion can only be a thing of beauty where it grows. You cannot put it into a vase or make it part of a posy of other flowers. So many of us want to be what we are not. We think what a success of life we would make if only we were rich, or in different surroundings, or had other people's opportunities. Instead of wasting time day-dreaming, we ought to get on with living where we are and making the best use of the opportunities and talents we have.

God has a place and a purpose for each one of us. He has given us our own individual talents and abilities. We are all different and have a special task to do in God's service. Whether we be dandelions or roses, we are important to God.

Matthew 10:31